Living
Peace

*To Sarah,
I hope the words in this book touch your heart + mind in meaningful ways.
Peace!,
Karen*

410-551-2703

Living
Peace

KAREN J. FOX

AuthorHouse™
1663 Liberty Drive
Bloomington, IN 47403
www.authorhouse.com
Phone: 1-800-839-8640

© 2012 Karen J. Fox. All rights reserved.

No part of this book may be reproduced, stored in a retrieval system, or transmitted by any means without the written permission of the author.

Published by AuthorHouse   04/10/2012

ISBN: 978-1-4685-7325-1 (sc)
ISBN: 978-1-4685-7324-4 (hc)
ISBN: 978-1-4685-7326-8 (e)

Library of Congress Control Number: 2012905492

Any people depicted in stock imagery provided by Thinkstock are models, and such images are being used for illustrative purposes only.
Certain stock imagery © Thinkstock.

This book is printed on acid-free paper.

Because of the dynamic nature of the Internet, any web addresses or links contained in this book may have changed since publication and may no longer be valid. The views expressed in this work are solely those of the author and do not necessarily reflect the views of the publisher, and the publisher hereby disclaims any responsibility for them.

CONTENTS

Introduction xi

Chapter 1: Changing our Lives 1
Chapter 2: Forgiveness 6
Chapter 3: Confidence 25
Chapter 4: Compassion 45
Chapter 5: Gratitude 62
Chapter 6: Integrity 74

Conclusion 87
Acknowledgements 91

This book is dedicated to all who seek peace in their lives and in our world.

If there is to be peace in the world,
 there must be
 peace in the nations.

If there is to be peace in the nations,
 there must be
 peace in the cities.

If there is to be peace in the cities,
 there must be
 peace between neighbors.

If there is to be peace between neighbors,
 there must be
 peace in the home.

If there is to be peace in the home,
 there must be
 peace in the heart.

Lau Tze

INTRODUCTION

Living peacefully is a life-long journey. Most of us desire peaceful lives. Many of us struggle to live in a way that promotes peace and justice for all. This book represents my journey toward living a peaceful life—living peace.

The challenge of living peace is to respond to life reminding ourselves that we want to approach each situation we encounter with a peaceful mindset. We want to live from our hearts, feeling all of life, and responding to it with love. It takes checking our responses, making choices, challenging ourselves to change our ways of thinking and engaging. It takes courage and commitment. Living peace won't come to any of us instantly. The journey to inner peace is both challenging and beautiful. And, it is worth the effort!

When we work toward living peace on an individual level we promote peace in the world. We are all cells in the one body of humanity, sharing all of the resources and energy of Earth. We are an interconnected and complex system and everything we do in our own lives has an effect on all others. In this oneness of humanity, when we find peace within, and promote it to all through our own learning, we are living peace.

In pages that follow, we will examine five principles for living peacefully. Originating in the teachings of Dr. Mikao Usui, founder of the Reiki Method of Self Healing, they are the result of years of meditation and work I have engaged in to find a deeper understanding of peace in my own life. These five principles come from my personal journey, and I hope that they enrich yours.

The key to living peacefully is to allow peace to prevail in our own lives *now*—not to wish for it in the future. By wishing for peace instead of living it we put it out of reach. We will never achieve a peaceful life by wishing for it—only by living it—*by living peace*.

CHAPTER 1

Changing our Lives

I am a Reiki Master/Teacher. Reiki is a complementary healing art introduced by Mikao Usui in the late 1800's. Dr. Usui was a sage. His dream was to help people connect with Spirit/Truth/Universal Life Force. Drawing upon the writings of the Meiji Emperor, who lived at the same time he did, Usui adopted the following principles to help his students understand a way to live a fruitful life.

The principles were:

- Do not anger.
- Do not worry.
- Be grateful.
- Be kind.
- Do an honest day's work.

These principles have been through many translations and iterations. The one that I received when I first encountered them was the translation in the book, *A Complete Book of Reiki Healing,* by Gunther.[1]

- Just for today, do not anger.
- Just for today, do not worry.
- Just for today, be grateful for life's blessings
- Just for today, be kind to every living thing.
- Just for today, do an honest day's work.

I have worked with and taught Reiki since 1998. Throughout this time I have sought a deeper understanding of the principles. I have come through a progression of new wording until I came to what I consider to be the essence of the five principles for living peacefully. Because I would rather focus on positive action than on what I should *not* do, my first attempt was to play with the wording while trying to reduce the "don'ts" and, always, through the progression of my understanding, to keep the integrity of the message. At the time of my first attempt, I believed that these principles were instructing us to live in the present moment, with a positive approach to life.

I offered my first translation and presented the principles in the following words in 2005.

➤ In this moment, I look to the past with gratitude for the people who have crossed my path and the lessons I have learned. (Do not anger.)
➤ In this moment, I look forward in joyful anticipation of what is yet to come. (Do not worry.)
➤ In this moment, I am grateful for all of the blessings of life. (Be grateful.)
➤ In this moment my thoughts, words, and actions, are grounded in kindness and compassion. (Be kind.)
➤ In this moment, I do my work, whatever it may be, with honor, honesty, and integrity. (Do an honest day's work.)

And I added:

➤ In this moment, in every moment, these are my intentions for living a full and fruitful life.

Later, when meditating on these principles, it became clear to me that they are really very simple. What exactly is it to not be angry? What can we do instead of being angry? Forgive! So it is in our best interest to move from anger into forgiveness. We are always being told not to worry, but what do we do with that energy? Have confidence! We are best served by turning the key or ribbon of our thinking from worry to confidence. The remaining three principles stay the same: Living in gratitude for all of the blessings and challenges of life; acting in kindness and compassion toward all beings; and having integrity in every moment. The five principles can each be spoken in one or two words.

- Forgive.
- Have confidence.
- Be grateful.
- Be kind and compassionate.
- Have integrity.

They make a wonderful mantra for meditation. I forgive; I have confidence; I am filled with gratitude; I am kind and compassionate; I am living a life of integrity. If they are repeated several times in preparation for meditation, or simply in preparation for your day, they can quiet the mind and help set the intention for the day. They can bring a sense of peace.

In fact, living by these principles can bring your life into alignment so that you can live peacefully, in the moment, appreciating life, people, circumstances, and lessons.

In every moment of every day we have a choice. We can live from a place of fear, mistrust, anger, and all of the emotions that go with fear. Or we can choose to live from an attitude of love, forgiving, having confidence in ourselves, our belief systems, other people, and in our own discernment. This is living peacefully.

This is important wisdom for our times. There is so much anger and fear in our world today that it is getting in the way of our true wisdom. A wonderful aspect of living peace is that, by changing our own lives, and through recognizing the interconnectedness of all of human beings, we also help lift humanity to a higher state of being. At the very least we improve the chances of finding our way to peaceful existence on earth.

CHAPTER 2

Forgiveness

Forgiveness unbinds us. It frees the energy we waste ruminating over the un-forgiven person or event, to be used in positive ways. It allows us to transmute negative energy into the energy of love. To forgive is to allow our Self to feel comfortable in the presence of others, including the person toward whom we have born a grievance.

True forgiveness erases the negative feelings that tend to arise when we are in the presence of an individual we believe has wronged us. It does not eradicate the memory of the event. We retain the wisdom and learning achieved through the experience, and release ourselves from negative or defensive reactions. When we have let anger go, we have moved one more step toward a state of being in oneness and understanding. Sometimes the anger will raise its head again at an unexpected time, even when we believe we have already done the work of forgiving. When this occurs we simply do the work of forgiving again.

The act of forgiving challenges the ego—that which separates us from our Source and our understanding of oneness. We overcome separation and are able to extend love to all beings.

Peace begins with forgiveness.

While anger is an important tool, and natural reaction that is a warning to fight or flee, carrying it and allowing it to fester in our hearts and minds does not serve us. When we are angry we are spurred to take action—to get out of the situation or to protect ourselves. In this context, anger is a helpful and useful tool. It becomes a problem when it is held onto and becomes irritation, resentment, or hatred.

Forgiveness is the greatest gift we can give ourselves. Carrying within our beings the pebbles or the boulders of anger, whether toward ourselves or toward others, is one of the most harmful energies we can hold. It is self-destructive to continue to carry this discordant energy. It can cause physical symptoms of headaches, ulcers, and other pain. It can also be one of the causes of depression. (Just so we won't have to go through the internal argument, I am not saying that it causes *all* ulcers, headaches, pain or depression.) As you learn to practice forgiveness you may find, as I did, that anger is causing symptoms that you didn't even realize were there.

Forgiveness can be easy or difficult. It can be very challenging to think about forgiving someone who has harmed us. Thinking about it seems to bring the event into our consciousness and bring up the anger. Often, as we repeatedly think about an event or a person that we need to forgive, the incident seems to get larger and more difficult to consider forgiving—and more harmful to our being. It is especially hard on us to hold anger for a long time. In many cases, this long-held anger will surface after extended periods of dormancy and will erupt from us in ways that we don't understand. The more time we allow to lapse between a hurtful event and releasing it in forgiveness, the more difficult forgiving seems to become. When we hold onto anger in its form of resentment, hate, or fear, the stories we tell ourselves about the harm done to us are what we ruminate about, resulting in the anger reaction. When the opportunity to forgive arises, amazingly enough, it's not all that difficult. We simply allow ourselves to let go and forgive. It is such a relief when it's over. Sometimes the same anger arises again. When that happens we just keep forgiving and letting go until the job of forgiveness is complete.

What are the reasons for not forgiving? Anger is such an uncomfortable energy to carry. It becomes a part of us, and we don't recognize the discomfort or discord we are holding in our beings. The point is that we carry this anger, this seed of discordant energy around with us and *we believe that it somehow serves us*. Ask yourself why you haven't forgiven someone who has hurt you in the past. Choose someone who did something that irritated you and you just seem to enjoy staying angry. What does that do for you?

When we think of the person or people we are angry with, what is it that we feel? It is anger, yes, and anger is a fear-based response. Along with the anger we are carrying fear that we may be hurt again, fear that we will be reminded of the incident when we see the person, that we will relive the situation. But how does it serve us? Do we feel that we are somehow better than the person we are angry with? Does it feed our ego? Does it give us an adrenalin rush when we see them and remember our anger? Or do we see ourselves as victims and does that somehow feed us? Our anger must serve us in some way or we wouldn't carry it. This is true no matter what the grievance is, whether it is anger resulting from something extreme that caused us deep harm physically, emotionally, or spiritually, or whether it's a result of something as upsetting as theft, or of something more minor like an unkindness. If we are not forgiving the person whose actions have in some way harmed us, we may think we have power over them. In truth we are giving away our power. We are giving away a part of our self by not forgiving them. They have a hold on us and we are allowing them to keep us in a place of discord. By not forgiving them, we have allowed them to go on hurting us over and over again. Even if it is not their desire or intention, they have a hold on us that will not be released until we release ourselves through forgiveness.

How would forgiveness serve us better? I can speak of my own experience here. Meditation has been a tool for me for many years. When meditating, I often take a look at my emotions—what am

I feeling? Not long ago I was leading a guided group meditation. We were exploring forgiveness and were invited to go inside and look around to see if we had anything to forgive. As I searched my consciousness, I found a small orange, almond-shaped object. I immediately thought of an early, significant relationship, and a person who wore an orange sweater, who had hit me on the shoulder. That shoulder and arm had been painful for over thirty years and I couldn't explain why. I had forgotten about the incident many years ago. It wasn't the physical injury that was causing the current pain. I was holding a grudge—I had a "chip on my shoulder"! In this meditation the entire incident was played out before me. My pain (both physical and emotional) became more intense as I relived the incident and my reaction to it. I gained an understanding that this anger wasn't serving me in any way. By envisioning that I smashed that orange almond, representing anger, with a sledge hammer, and that a cool wind blew the pieces away, I dismissed the feelings about the incident that I'd been carrying for years. I still needed to release the anger and fear held against the person. I asked Spirit[2] for assistance and guidance to forgive the individual and, while sitting in silence, I let the discordant energy melt away. In that moment, I was able to truly forgive the person and let go of the fear-based energy of anger. The person has not been a part of my life for many years. I cannot talk with them about the incident, but I can forgive and let go. I know that if I encounter them, I will be confident, not traumatized by the memory of an incident that no longer matters and no longer has control over me.

Later the same week I got a massage. In the past that shoulder was tight and painful. Now, for the first time in years, the shoulder pain was completely gone. It has remained healed. This is significant healing. The pain and tightness have not returned. I needed to forgive in order to heal my spirit and my body.

I invite you to take a close look. How does anger serve you? Does it really help you in any meaningful way? What is its purpose? Do you think it protects you? How? Do you think it makes you more vigilant for the next time someone tries to hurt you? Or does it make you feel less trusting? How does being less trusting, more suspicious, serve you in the long run? Does it really serve you to live in fear?

Many of us have at least one person toward whom we carry anger because it serves us by allowing us to feel as if we are, in some way, better than they are. When this is present for me, it helps to remember something my mentor once said. He said that we are all on our own perfect journeys toward enlightenment and peace. Each of us is in a different place on that journey, learning a different lesson. The important thing to remember is that we are each exactly where we need to be on that journey, learning what we need to learn in the moment. When we remember this, we can let go of feeling superior because we, in the past have been, or in the future will be, learning that same lesson at some point on our own journey!

It is not only the offender that is released in forgiveness, but often more importantly, the person forgiving. In fact, often the offender has gone on with their life, forgetting, sometimes even unaware, that they have offended or harmed us. Or perhaps they forgave themselves long ago! They have no idea that we are walking around carrying this grievance and anger toward them. We have given them power over us that they aren't aware of, and most likely, don't want. While we are harming ourselves carrying this anger and discord within, they are living their life, unaware. Have you ever talked to someone with the intention of forgiving them and had them say to you that they had no idea they had done whatever it was that hurt you? Now that you've told them, they are sorry for the offense. They have been living their life completely unaffected while you have been living in a state of discord, maybe even suffering over the event. How much better it would serve us to address events when they happen. "Using I statements,"[1] to tell the person how they have hurt us, asking for

---

[1] To use an "I statement" is to say something like, "when you did (insert the action that is bothering you) I felt (insert your feelings) rather than "you made me feel _____ when you _____."

change, *taking responsibility for our feelings, and forgiving even if an apology is not offered and forgiveness is not sought.*

Forgiveness is a challenge that faces us nearly every day in life. There are constant opportunities to forgive. The person cutting us off in traffic, the rude clerk at the store, the angry person in line, and the family member who did something irritating, are all offering us an opportunity to practice forgiving and letting go. Each time, we make a choice to either forgive or to carry the grudge in our body, mind, and spirit. We can choose to poison our being and let little grievances build throughout the day until we are angry and we're not even sure why. The muscles in the back of our neck and shoulders are tight. There's a knot in our stomach. Maybe we experience heart burn. We begin to snap at our co-workers, or our friends and family. All of this, because we let the anger build up, instead of choosing in each moment to let it go.

In instances where anger is a result of abuse, we need to listen to the fight or flee message of anger. It is important to remove ourselves from situations where we are abused in any way, physically, emotionally, or mentally. Getting out of the situation comes *before* forgiveness.

While "I statements" are not appropriate in all of the above mentioned situations, forgiveness is. Sometimes it's helpful to simply understand that the offender is having a rough day. To forgive each small incident keeps us in a state of balance. Then, when something important comes up we are ready to meet it in a more objective and even way. We can meet each moment with compassion and understanding, rather than with the toxic energy of the accumulated grievances, that would have built up if we had not been in a state of forgiveness throughout the day.

By engaging in forgiveness, we free both the person with whom we are angry and ourselves. We begin to heal ourselves and the whole of humanity. We do not live in a vacuum. When we improve our own spiritual health we incrementally improve the whole of the interdependent web of humanity of which we are a part.

So how do we forgive? How do we let go? Forgiveness is simply a decision to no longer carry the anger and fear that were a response to a fear-producing interaction or incident. The fear in the instant of the incident was a red flag, a warning to take action. When we make the decision to carry that anger, or resentment, or fear with us into the future we are harming ourselves. Especially harmful is the decision to stay rather than flee an abusive situation.

Every time we bring an anger-provoking incident to the surface and allow it to cause ill feelings we are giving away our power again and again. One way to access the ability to let go of our anger and fear is to put our self in the shoes of the person who we perceive has injured us in some way. Did they cut us off in traffic because they were late—or because they were taking a personal action against us? Are they a person who has been physically hurt by loved ones and knows no other way to express their frustration or anger? Are they themselves so hurt and angry that they don't know that they're hurting others?

Of course, none of this makes whatever they have done okay, but it helps to give us a different window through which to view the incident. Looking or observing through this window of understanding, we can see that the action was probably not intended to hurt us. We struggle because we have taken an action or word personally. As Miguel Ruiz says in his book *The Four Agreements*,[3] "don't take anything personally because by taking things personally you set yourself up to suffer for nothing." If we practice this understanding of not taking anything personally, we will have much less to forgive. We won't be hurt or upset. If we don't take another's words or actions personally, there is nothing to forgive because we have not been affronted!

Reflections on My Journey with Forgiveness

Anger can sometimes seem to serve us well. There is a person in my life against whom, until recently, I have carried lots of anger for many years. My anger served me in many ways. I sometimes felt superior to this individual. Other times I just wanted to say things about them behind their back, to gossip. Why did I engage anger in this way? It gave me something to talk about when I was with other people who were angry at the same person. It allowed me to watch for any action that could spur my anger. I was embedded in bitterness and anger that I didn't even see. I felt better than this individual in many ways. I actually felt, in a competitive way, that I was more compassionate than this person was! This was most certainly not a love-based response to the person, or the situations we shared in life!

By doing all of this, I was engaging in a kind of self-destruction. By not forgiving this person, by watching for things that I could use to spur my anger, I was hurting myself. I was damaging my ability to love unconditionally, to have compassion for what another person's life has rendered for them. By deciding to be bitter and angry I was making sure that I wouldn't enjoy this person when I was in their presence. What a mess I was making, and what power I was giving away!

It is very easy to slip into the irrationality of resentment-based behavior—to engage in behind the scenes discussions about someone—to gossip. I am not proud of how long I engaged in this behavior or how long it took me to listen to the advice I had given so many others.

When I finally did the work of forgiving, it took quite some time. I had not realized just how much anger I had stored up. Not only did I have to do the work of forgiving this person, I had to forgive myself for engaging in years of harmful thoughts, unkind words, and hurtful ideas. I was not living up to my own standards of forgiveness and compassion. I was not asking the important questions about why this person hurt so much that they hurt others. I was wallowing in my anger and sharing it with others who were also angry. Together we were complicit in creating a bitterness that was harmful to carry.

As I contemplated how to forgive, how to free myself from this negativity, I finally asked myself this question. "If anger is a fear-based response, what am I afraid of in this relationship?" The answer didn't come easily, and I'm not proud of what came forth. I was a little afraid that another person would ridicule me for forgiving. I was more than a little afraid that the person would continue to do things that are hurtful. And, I was afraid that if I forgave, I would no longer feel superior. These, I know, seem small minded, and they are. It was my job, as a person trying to establish peace in my world and in the world we share, to follow my own guidance, to let it all go and forgive both myself and the person toward whom I carried such discord. I had to forgive myself for reacting to things with resentment instead of trying to understand, and for magnifying anger by talking about this person with another person who was also enjoying our anger.

I had to forgive many events with the person toward whom I carried all of this anger. You see, I had been keeping score for a long time, and when I asked myself what made me mad I came up with many examples. What I didn't recognize was that years ago I had decided to be angry, and there was nothing this person could do to assuage my anger. The only person who could release the anger was me. I had to own it, own how unhealthy and unhelpful it was, and forgive. I needed to forgive myself for such erroneous thinking, and forgive the person for acts that came to mind that had elicited my anger in the first place. I had to release each instance of anger. This person was undoubtedly unaware of all the times I had become angry. This discord was my own doing. Yes, they might well repeat something in the future that has made me angry in the past. Perhaps if I had honestly communicated why I was upset, the actions wouldn't come up again. Perhaps I would have been able to recognize my own complicit behavior feeding my anger.

As I did the work of forgiveness and letting go, I used meditation, a bowl of water, and some stones. I brought to mind memories and incidents that I carried—some I'd carried for years. As I forgave each incident that came to mind, I dropped a stone in the water, symbolically cleansing myself of this discordant energy. This person doesn't know that I was carrying such animosity toward them. I have not seen this individual for a while, but our paths cross in life. I am sure though, that the fact that I have done this work will make me more comfortable being with this individual in the future. I will be more relaxed, more comfortable in my own skin, and I won't be watching, expecting something to feed my anger. I will be in genuine conversation and interaction. I anticipate that time together will be easier, more meaningful, and actually nourishing. I know that things may come up that anger me again. It will be my challenge to continue to forgive. It is not the other person that has needed to change. It is me, and my response to their actions or words.

Another challenge will be to stand in my own integrity when I spend time with the other person who also carries anger toward this individual. I will, in truthfulness and integrity, require myself to talk about the work and benefit of forgiving. In honoring my own integrity, I will decide not to engage in the down-talking gossip, but to talk about how carrying this anger has harmed me and how forgiving has changed my outlook. It's a risk to my relationship with this person, but I have confidence that we will both grow as we process our conversation.

I disclosed this very personal story in hopes of several things. One is to acknowledge that I'm not perfect. None of us is able to live to our highest potential in every moment. Life is a journey of learning and I still have my own work to do. More importantly, it gives a very specific example of how poorly we are served by carrying grudges. The action of carrying resentments and anger brings out the meanness in us. It feeds a part of us that we, and our world, would be better served by healing.

As I reflect on having taken this opportunity to truly forgive I feel lighter. I am no longer anticipating the next thing that will feed my anger. I am confident that I have moved past the need to feel superior, to gossip, and to fear ridicule because I've done the work of forgiving.

It's interesting to me that I've had less difficulty forgiving the big hurts in life, and have experienced so much challenge in forgiving people for the little affronts. I have taken very personally the things that I allowed to feed my anger. I have held onto them, nurtured the resentment, and felt avenged in gossiping and feeling superior. In truth, even though the anger seemed to feed me, none of this has served me in any way. In fact, it has stunted my spiritual growth as I have not released what needed so badly to be let go of. And yet, I held on to the bitterness and anger. I am relieved to have let go now.

I am reminded of many years ago when someone I was confiding in about other, bigger anger gave me some very poor advice. Maybe you've received it too. The suggestion was that I put all of the anger into a little box and imagine putting it in a closet somewhere in the back of my mind. This meant I would carry the anger forever, never doing the work of forgiving, and never allowing myself to heal. I hope that you have not received such advice. If you are carrying around pain caused by incidents in your life, hoping to never have to address them again, I invite you to bring out the box, open it, and let the contents go. You can use the method of the stones and water, you can write the grievances down and burn the paper, you can find another meaningful way to let go. But letting go is very important for your health and for your inner peace, just as it has been for mine.

Clarissa Pinkola Estés, in her book, *Women Who Run with the Wolves*[4], states that there are four stages to forgiveness. First is to forego; to walk away or remove ourselves from the incident for a while. In this way we give ourselves time to cool off, to remember the truth of who we are. Second is to forebear; abstain from taking action as a result of our anger, giving us time to consider what actions we might take. Third is to forget; to refuse to dwell on the incident, not to forget the incident and its lessons, but to release the emotions attached to it. And finally, fourth is to forgive; this is the release of the incident, allowing us to move forward. We don't give up the incident, we create space to release it and move forward in our lives while retaining the lessons learned through the experience.

When I finally did the work of forgiving the above mentioned person, it was important for me to take some time out and forego reacting to the situations that inspired my rage. When I was able to stop myself from the action of engaging in rage, talking about it, or looking for more; when I was able to allow myself to stop dwelling on the incidents and realize that they were in the past and it didn't serve me to continue my patterns of dwelling in anger and resentment, I was finally able to let it all go, and to forgive the person. I was able to forgive myself for continuing to carry anger and bitterness. That is when peace with the situation was finally possible. My anger gave this individual power over my emotions. I was giving myself away in a self-destructive way. By practicing the action of forgiveness, I have freed myself from the discordant, harmful emotions that I was forcing myself to carry.

I have found peace in remembering this person and my relationship with them, bringing a deeper and more sustainable peace to my own life.

Reflections on Your Journey with Forgiveness

_____
_____
_____
_____
_____
_____
_____
_____
_____
_____
_____
_____
_____
_____
_____
_____
_____

"Forgiving is not having to understand. Understanding may come later, in fragments, an insight here and a glimpse there, after forgiving."

LEWIS SMEEDES

Karen J. Fox

CHAPTER 3

Confidence

> *Confidence in Self allows us to follow our own inner guidance. It enables us to move forward in life with self-assurance, with courage, and with vision.*
>
> *Confidence in others comes with a sense that they are who and what they represent themselves to be. We have confidence in their integrity, allowing us to engage or interact with them.*
>
> *Confidence in our understanding of our Source, God, Spirit or the Universe is trust in something greater than all and a part of each. This enhances our sense of security, our strength, and our wisdom.*
>
> *Confidence in an outcome resulting from our actions, either alone or with others, gives us the ability to plan, to move forward, and to have hope.*
>
> *Confidence is the transformational way out of worry. We are often admonished not to worry about something or someone when we are actually feeling anxious, apprehensive, or fearful of an outcome. The suggestion here is to let go of anxiety and fear—to have confidence in yourself, in the others involved, and in the outcome.*
>
> **Confidence helps us transform our state of mind to one of peace.**

When I originally honed Dr. Usui's principles into one-word statements, I thought the principle "do not worry" would become "trust". Over time I've had many discussions about the challenges of trust and who to trust, what to trust, and how to trust. In addition there were questions about what to do when trust is broken. I have come to the conclusion that having confidence is a more appropriate and accessible idea. This is confidence in ourselves, in what we know and understand about other people, in our approach to understanding Spirit, or Source, or God, or in not believing in those paradigms. When we have confidence in an outcome we can take action. Confidence depends upon self-esteem, an understanding of our strengths and weaknesses, our vulnerabilities, and our possibilities.

When we are admonished not to worry about something or someone, rarely are we given a suggestion of what to do with the feelings and the energy that go with the state of worry. We need to have a constructive way to turn that energy around and make it positive—a way to get out of the state of anxiety.

I would like to suggest that worry takes us out of the present moment and into the future. We cannot control the future, that's why we engage in worry. Let's use an example that is familiar to most people. If you have had the experience of a loved one being in need of urgent medical care, you have probably engaged in worry. When we are worried about a loved one who is undergoing surgery or experiencing a health crisis, we are looking ahead with deep concern about the future results of whatever is happening right now. We are afraid that the outcome will not be positive. Our worry won't change the outcome or be of any benefit to the person or situation we are anxious about. And it's certainly not helping us! If we remove ourselves from the state of anxiety, and transform that energy into positive feelings of hope and confidence, we can offer more effective support to our loved one.

Worry freezes us—shuts us down. When we're anxious it's difficult to think clearly, to plan, or to expect a positive outcome. If we take that energy of worry, turn it around, and instead use it to embrace confidence, we will have more peace of mind. Confidence is defined as assurance, a sense of self reliance or boldness. If we turn the worry, fear, and anxiety in any situation, around into one of confident expectation, we are engaging in positive thinking. This can have a significant influence on our ability to cope with difficult situations. Confidence can also give us the energy to think of ways to change the situation or to plan constructively for whatever the outcome may be. In the situation above, confidence could be placed in the medical professionals helping our loved one; confidence that God or Source will guide the outcome for the highest good; confidence in our loved one's ability and strength to heal; confidence in our own ability to be able to offer whatever assistance will be needed, during recovery. We could place confidence in our ability to cope with the outcome, whatever it may be. Because we are not privy to the highest good for another person's life, confidence that the outcome is for their highest good can bring a sense of peace about what is happening.

Another aspect of confidence is allowing others into our lives in order to create relationships built on respect, understanding, caring, and concern. Sometimes we find it very difficult to trust anyone because of the way we have been treated in the past. In this case, we need to look carefully at the person we are considering letting into our lives and ask ourselves if they are sincere, reliable, and competent—if they have the traits we are looking for in this relationship. If, after observation and interaction with this new person, we are confident that they have the traits we are looking for, we can feel assured that we can trust them. This is discernment of the potential for safety.

An area where people often lack confidence is in dealing with institutions like the government, churches, or public services. Our personal histories are often the source of our lack of confidence. It is difficult to trust when we have been injured by individuals or by representatives of agencies. Often that fear or worry, that anxiety caused by patterns in our past with others, is expanded to the mistrust of people or agencies with whom we don't even have a history. We need to ask ourselves if this person or institution has our best interest at heart. Asking ourselves, in any situation, if those we are interacting with are worthy of our confidence in their abilities, helps us to discern if they are the appropriate choice in our endeavor. Often, research is required, and we must discover the trustworthiness of individuals, companies, or agencies according to what our investigation shows us. As I write this, I am trying to find a good self-publishing company. I need to discern whether the agency is trustworthy, if their product is what I want this book to look like, if they have integrity in how they will protect my work, handle compensation, advertise, and other aspects of their work. I am finding this challenging because I've never done it before. Asking other people who have experience about companies they've used, what questions they've asked, and what packages worked for them, I can make a more confident decision.

Confidence is a safety issue. If our life history is one where we have consistently felt cared for and safe, where we have been able to express ourselves without fear, and where we have felt honored and respected, it is much easier for us to have confidence that we will be treated respectfully and fairly. I don't know anyone who hasn't had at least one experience in life that would encourage them to worry, or to be afraid that people or organizations will try to take advantage of them. It takes work to re-establish confidence. Sometimes we have to start out slowly and allow trust to develop over time as we have better experiences. Trusting always involves some level of risk taking. Using the observations above, we must discern whether this is a good risk, or we are taking a risk that is unwise.

So what happens to our thinking when we make decisions based on confidence, and the outcome is still not what we hoped for? What happens when we have done the work and decided to trust in someone and then are taken advantage of? Do we decide to never trust again? This is the answer that some individuals rely on. "I've been hurt too many times to ever trust anyone again." They have become confident that they will be hurt again. Developing confidence is a positive action. It requires that we recognize that our fear and distrust separates us from the love of others, from the ability to love ourselves, and from our ability to accept shared wisdom. If we can accept and have confidence in others and enjoy their presence in our lives, we will experience a life that is more rich and full. By accepting others, we will also be accepted by them, and they will have confidence in us.

It is essential for us to develop a sense that life is fair, that most people are good and would never want to do us harm. Developing this confidence requires us to take risks, to become vulnerable, to let go of fear. This can be very challenging. The first person to have confidence in is our Self. We must be sure of our own judgment about who we can trust. Having a strong sense of self, and belief in our competency of discernment, is essential to developing trust in others.

Confidence is the step that follows forgiveness. Once we have done the work of forgiving another person or ourselves, we develop confidence that the same thing won't happen again. We have confidence that we will be able to prevent the situation from recurring, and we have confidence in the other person to not repeat the offense. We also have confidence that, should the incident be repeated, we have the required skill to deal with it.

It is often stated that trust must be earned. This way of thinking keeps us always on the defensive. What if we decide to have confidence in people's integrity until they give us a reason not to? What if we lived our lives in a way that *distrust* was what had to be earned? How would that change our interactions with others? We would expect others to trust us. We would expect others to be trustworthy. We would not be living in the fear and anxiety that others are out to get us, or that we could be harmed by anyone at any time. We would be engaging life in a positive and confident way. We would be moving forward with confidence and the expectation that all is well instead of being anxious that bad things will happen.

I am by nature a very trusting person. Yes, I have had bad things happen in my life—things that might lead a person to be mistrustful of others. But I've had more good experiences than bad. I enjoy being with other people so much that living in a state of anxiety and fear that someone might harm me would make it impossible for me to live the life that I lead. In fact, it was during those times in my life when I was mistrustful of others that more unfortunate events took place. People had to earn my trust. Because I was not confident in others or in myself, I was drawing to myself people who were not trustworthy. I was looking for what I couldn't trust—and I found it! At some point I made the decision that I did not want to live in fear of people. I began to use more careful discernment of who was worthy of my confidence, asking the questions above. I then began expecting to be surrounded by those I could trust. Once I started expecting people to be trustworthy, I was, and still am, surrounded by people who I honor and respect and they return those feelings to me.

Another area of confidence that is very important to our sense of personal safety is whether we can trust That Which Is Greater Than All and a Part of Each, God, Spirit, Universe, The Divine in whatever way we define it. If we believe in something that is greater than ourselves, we must be able to have confidence in its existence. We must be able to have trust in the guidance that we receive from our connection with that power. Confidence in our belief system, no matter what it is, becomes one of the most important aspects of inner peace. Ultimately, it is not as important what we believe as it is that we have confidence in that belief. If one is an atheist, they must have a deep confidence in the belief that there is not a higher power to turn to. We must trust ourselves and what we know within ourselves to be true. Whatever we hold to be true, we are most secure in our belief system if we have enough confidence to question what we believe. Trying on something new and deciding if it fits, changing our beliefs as we grow, and exploring new ways of belief are part of having confidence in our ability to discern what deeply nourishes us. Any belief system that we embrace should be true to our authentic selves, to the deepest, most private and inner aspects of our thinking, our motivations in life, and our expressions of what we believe.

The law of attraction was recently being talked about almost everywhere we turned. It tells us that we create or draw to us that which we think about, and to which we give our energy. When I was looking for what I could not trust in people, I was, according to this law, attracting people I could not trust. When I began looking for those I could have confidence in, I began to draw safe, nurturing, supportive and honest people into my life.

Hope is the result of confidence. If we trust ourselves, our friends, and our beliefs, we have positive expectations for the future. Self-confidence allows us to trust our own actions, our ability to discern positive, loving energy from fearful energy. Our ability to choose appropriate people to work or be with, and our confidence to speak our own truth, is essential to our ability to reach out and engage in life. It allows us to trust our own decisions. We have peace in our hearts that can then permeate our home, our lives, and our world. In this way we can have a positive effect on all of humanity through our interconnected relationships to one another. In our oneness, we are having an uplifting effect on all.

Reflections on My Journey with Confidence

In my reflections on forgiveness I stated that once I was able to forgive the person against whom I carried so much rage for so many years, I found confidence. Because of finding this confidence I am sure that when I am with the person again I will be more comfortable in my own skin, more compassionate, more whole. I also know from experience that I will be careful about placing my trust in them again. I will wait, watch, listen, and discern when it is appropriate to trust again. Should an incident take place that causes me to be angry in the moment, I will confront the situation and deal with it with confidence, speaking my truth. The confidence gained from what I have learned will make it easier for me to move forward.

There are other aspects of confidence that are also important in living peacefully. As with all of the principles, trust in our

Selves must come first. I struggled with trusting my abilities for many years. I, like many other women my age, had a high school counselor who told me that I "wasn't college material." She indicated that I should plan on trade school because I'd never make it in college. At the time this was said to me, I was carrying some dreams that would require a college education. I wanted to be a designer, either of clothing or of the interiors of homes, apartments, and offices. I was all too willing to accept the authority of a woman who didn't know anything about me other than the letters on a page that indicated I wasn't great in math and had a hard time learning a foreign language. I was young, 17 or so. I didn't have the confidence to say to her that I wanted to work hard so I could go to college. I didn't have the confidence in myself to believe that I had it in me to succeed. I did take the chance of going to an art institute to check it out. One of the questions asked by the admissions counselor was, "Are you a loner?" My answer was honest and I said that I enjoy being with other people. It wasn't a qualified answer. If I had been thinking about when I was drawing, creating, making art, I would have said that I liked to be alone for that. This thought didn't occur to me for many years. The admissions counselor's response was that I would never make it in art school if I liked being with people. At that, I gave up my dreams. That easily, I walked away from my hopes.

I was determined to do *something* so I went to cosmetology school and became a hair stylist. After graduating and working as a hair dresser for a couple of years, I realized that this was not my passion. I'd had enough. I decided to try the local junior college. Doing very well there improved my self-confidence. This brought a sense of confidence that I had not experienced before. I even did very well in the science classes that I took. Learning a foreign language was still challenging, but I managed to succeed at that too.

I finally remembered years later that one of the dreams I had carried since junior high school was that I would become a writer. I had deeply buried that dream and only remembered it years after attaining my bachelor's degree and working in an unrelated field. Now I am living that dream while also working with a small non-profit in the community where I live, and offering Reiki sessions and workshops. Life has brought me the opportunities to develop trust in my mind, in my strength, in my abilities, and in the Source of my being. I have the confidence to write this book that, I hope, will make a difference in people's lives.

As I sit writing this, the musical, "The sound of Music," comes to mind. Maria, the main character, is singing about confidence. "I have confidence in confidence alone. Besides which, you see, I have confidence in me!" She has this great sense of confidence in spite of the questions and doubts of the nuns, and in spite of her own fears. If you remember the musical you will recall her angst as she tried to make decisions. She cried, she worried, and she wondered what was right. The nun told her to take risks and trust herself and she learned to do just that. She created the life that she desired by trusting her feelings and making decisions. She trusted her discernment about Professor Von Trapp, and she moved forward into the life she desired—with its own set of challenges.

Interestingly, I saw that movie at the same time that I was tossing my own confidence to the wind because of what that counselor had told me. No wonder I still remember it so well!

I changed as I grew, and continue to grow and change now. I recognize opportunities to make decisions that will nurture my life and my ability to trust myself and those around me. I learned to discern whether I can trust knowledge that is presented to me. As I move through life with confidence that I am able to discern the truth of any situation—even if that discernment requires research and investigation—I continue to live a life that is more fulfilling than the one I was willing to accept when my confidence was low. Once I learned that I could have confidence in myself, I moved forward to learn to trust others.

Everyone has been betrayed in at least some small way. I have been hurt by relationships, just as many others have. I have been let down when I had expectations that people would behave in a certain way and didn't. I have been injured by the actions of others.

The very experiences that have hurt me in the past are the ones that have taught me discernment. Each of those painful experiences taught me something about myself and about when to trust others. One good resource for discerning trustworthiness is listening. When people talk I listen carefully for hints about their trustworthiness. I have learned through a combination of positive and negative experiences in life, to discern whether what people say rings true. I have learned to trust my own instincts regarding their integrity.

Life has brought me opportunities to develop trust in my mind, in my strength, in my abilities, and in my Source. The final aspect of learning to have confidence is that of learning to trust the Source of our Being, God, Goddess, Spirit, the Universe, or whatever other way that which is a part of all and greater than each is named. This confidence is crucial to the ability to move through life with a sense of sureness.

I know that some people disagree with this belief. I also know that non-believers know that their lives are not entirely in their own control. I am talking here about the ability to have confidence in the core of my own being. If this Source is a part of each and greater than all, as I believe it is, it has some kind of influence on everything around me. This is difficult to explain because I don't believe in judgment or punishment from this Source. For me this Source is the basic energy of pure love, and of life. Therefore, my trust is in a loving energy that is part of all and greater than each. For me, that energy is the glue that holds the universe or universes together. It is when that energy of Spirit meets the energy of matter that life occurs. It doesn't matter what life, all life is the result of this union. So my confidence lies in the purest, most powerful love I can imagine. I trust that if I look within to discern the right actions to take, I am looking to that spark of light that is the connection between the physical matter that is my body, and the pure love that is my Source. It is here that I place my deepest trust.

Those of you who have a different belief system than mine also have developed some kind of trust in what you believe. Look to your life and decide whether this belief system supports your highest good. If it does, trust it. Embrace it with your whole heart.

Let me tell you a little about how I came to this belief system. We all have a spiritual journey of some kind, and sometimes hearing someone else's journey helps us to understand our own. I grew up in a Christian home. My family loved me. My parents followed the best advice they had available to them and taught me what they believed. When I was a young woman I decided to leave this religion and explore others. I stumbled around for a while. First I was just not interested in any religion at all. I stayed in that mind set for many years. Then, when I had children I wanted to develop a community they could trust. I did what many others do and turned to the church. My husband and I chose the Unitarian Universalist church where we live. The beliefs there are broad enough and embrace differences in belief systems, and that makes us feel more comfortable going there. Through that church, I was introduced to a women's spirituality group exploring the divine feminine. I checked into it and have been a member of it for over 20 years.

The group has been a source of support and understanding, as well as a place where I can explore my beliefs. During that time, I have experienced life on disability for 10 years because of debilitating the migraines. I learned when I was 47 that I had a birth defect that was going to kill me within a few months if I didn't have surgery. The survival chance with that surgery was 50/50. I didn't hesitate to schedule surgery. During the time leading up to it I faced the possibility of death. I had a young family and a wonderful husband and certainly, in spite of the pain I was experiencing from the migraines, did not want to die just yet! I reviewed my life. It had been reasonably good so far, but I wanted more. I went through the work of questioning my understanding of God. I was angry for a little while and realized that anger was not helping me. I was supported on this journey of soul searching by the group of women mentioned earlier. I decided to place my trust in the outcome of my surgery in the energy of life that I define as Source. I was at peace when I went into the surgery. I knew that my life could end then and there. I went into the surgery with trust in my surgeon, trust in my own ability to survive, trust in my family, and trust in the Source of My Being, that the outcome would be for my highest good. I was very happy when I survived.

Hope was a part of the experience. I held on to a hope that I would make it through. My belief system did not, and does not assume that the hand of Source guided the surgery. My hope was placed in my surgeon and his team's skill and in my body's ability to heal. My faith that there is something greater than myself, that is a part of everything comforted me.

I realize that not everyone experiences such drastic circumstances, but every one of us has our faith—our confidence—tested many times in life. What have you learned about confidence in yourself? Where do you place your trust? Have you examined it to be sure that you are comfortable with it? If so, you have confidence in whatever it is that you understand to be God, Goddess, Spirit, The Universe, All That

Is. Continue to hone your belief system as life presents you with new challenges. Have confidence in your own ability to discern the wisdom that you need. Confidence allows us to question that in which we hold our deepest belief and to grow from the questioning.

Reflections on Your Journey with Confidence

"Hold the image of a slowly opening and unfolding flower. There is no need to wonder, 'Will that flower unfold?' Of course it will. That is its truth, its nature. Trust then, that your nature is unfolding as it is meant to unfold . . . there is nothing to be done but to accept this reality."

EMMANUEL

Karen J. Fox

CHAPTER 4

Compassion

The definition of the word compassion from its Latin roots is to "suffer with". But what is it to suffer? One definition is to abide; To remain faithful to, to stand with, or to support.

We begin with ourselves. To have compassion toward ourselves means that we remain faithful to ourselves as we recognize that we have failings or shortcomings. We are kind to ourselves as we find ways to gently change and transform what we are capable of changing now. We know that our growth is continual and that we will grow in our understanding of how to be more of what we want to be. Then we take compassion and kindness into the world.

Compassion for another does not mean to enter into their pain; it means to help them through it. We are able to support another person through difficulties without being encumbered by their burdens. Holding them with deep understanding and respect, and in kindness, we do what we are able to do to help them. At the same time we compassionately respect our own limits. If we, through misguided compassion or empathy, put our own well-being at serious risk we are simply adding to the problem. We must be responsible to ourselves and to the outcome for the person we are trying to help.

Our responsible acts of kindness and compassion return to us in the form of the joy of helping another. They return to us when we need assistance and another is compassionate toward us. It is a cycle, and it is beautiful.

A world filled with compassionate people is a world at peace.

Once, when I was talking with one of my mentors, I spoke of having great empathy for what a client of mine was experiencing. He said, rather firmly, that it was very important that I not take on another's suffering. If we engage in another's suffering, he said, we will "burn out"—use up all of our energy in feeling their pain. He strongly indicated that compassion was a better pathway to helping this person. I agree with this assessment. When I hold what a person is experiencing with deep understanding and truly connect with them in a way that they feel heard and cared for, I am much more likely to be helpful than I am if I take on their suffering. Truly hearing a person can help them to empower themselves to take appropriate steps out of the situation in which they find themselves. Identifying with their pain and taking it into our own beings can keep them stuck—and we can find ourselves stuck as well. This can actually result in undermining the individual's self-empowerment. In order to overcome their own life challenges and learn the lessons life offers they must have confidence *within* to change, whether it means they will change their situation or not.

Let's talk a little about what compassion is not. It is not pity or feeling sorry for someone. Pity often includes a sense of condescension, as well as feeling somewhat removed from the person and what they are going through. It can include an assumption that the person cannot take care of their situation.

We often hear or read a statement like, "I don't want your pity." That's because pity is not helpful. It keeps the downtrodden down. It causes a feeling of inferiority. When we have compassion for someone we are not looking down upon them, but seeing their burden and doing our best to empower them to move through their problem.

Compassion is not fixing the problem. This also dis-empowers the person we think we are helping. It takes away their ability to work through the issue, and it reduces their sense of autonomy and self-worth. This kind of action can actually prevent the individual from learning how to manage on their own, creating a sense of dependency on us.

Compassion is not taking on the problem. The act of taking on the problem again places us in a sense of superiority because we are taking on the burden of the other, which indicates that they cannot carry it themselves. We compassionately can stand with them and support them without being superior.

Compassion upholds *the individual's* integrity and sense of self while we do what we are able to do to work with them to bring about the change that they desire. In compassion we see the burden, understand, through communication, what is going on and how we can help as an equal. We can work with them to help them to move toward self-empowerment, discerning how to get through the challenge they face.

As we move through each day of our lives, we have many opportunities to express compassion. Again here, we must each begin with our individual Self. We must examine our own failings, weaknesses, mistakes, or disappointments with compassion for our Self. Understanding that each of these is an opportunity for learning and growth is a valuable tool for being compassionate toward ourselves. It is so easy to be judgmental toward ourselves when we feel that we have not measured up to our own or others' expectations. Having compassion toward ourselves means that we recognize that we are fallible; we notice that we can do things differently and work at changing. It doesn't mean self-deprecation or anger. Nor does it mean that we have to "tough through it" on our own. If we don't like the way we have reacted to a situation, we can apologize to those involved, forgive ourselves, and decide to behave differently the next time. We don't judge ourselves as bad or incompetent.

If we fail to reach a particular goal we have set for ourselves, we can look at what is holding us back and work at changing it. We can accept the assistance of another person who has had a similar experience, or is otherwise capable of standing with us, and helping us as we move through the challenge. Or it can mean that we accept our limitations and don't need to change because we have a new understanding of who we are. *The key is to be gentle with ourselves.* It is helpful to recognize our own efforts, to remember what it is that we do well, to honor our journey toward wholeness, and to recognize that this journey has bumps and potholes in the road. Compassion toward ourselves opens us to the ability to be compassionate toward others.

> *Compassion is what makes our lives meaningful. It is the source of all lasting happiness and joy. And it is the foundation of a good heart, the heart of one who acts out of a desire to help others. Through kindness, through affection, through honesty, through truth and justice toward all others we ensure our own benefit. This is not a matter for complicated theorizing. It is a matter of common sense. There is no denying that consideration of others is worthwhile. There is no denying that our happiness is inextricably bound up with the happiness of others. There is no denying that if society suffers, we ourselves suffer. Nor is there any denying that the more our hearts and minds are afflicted with ill-will, the more miserable we become. Thus we can reject everything else: religion, ideology, all received wisdom. But we cannot escape the necessity of love and compassion.*
>
> His Holiness, the Dalai Lama
Ethics for the New Millennium
Riverhead Books

In every interaction we can appreciate the person who is in front of us. We can appreciate their humanity, their work, their *being*. The way we treat each person with whom we interact has ramifications beyond the moment of our interaction. The way we treat each person in the present moment has a direct effect upon their next interaction, and upon ours. Ultimately it has consequences for the entire body of humanity.

When I suggest that we interact with others through kindness and compassion, I am actually suggesting that we hold them with deep understanding and respect, and, in kindness, do what we are able to do to support them. At the same time we must respect our own limits. If we, through misguided compassion or empathy, put our own well-being at serious risk, we are adding to the problem rather than helping anyone. I am not saying that we should not take risks. I'm saying that we must be responsible to ourselves and to the outcome for the person to whom we are offering compassionate support. Reasonable risks can be important in our acts of compassion. We may find ourselves taking a risk to trust someone, or to offer our own energy in helping. When we take appropriate risks in life, we grow from the experiences.

When we offer compassion we offer what is needed unconditionally—which means without expectations of a specific outcome or repayment. Just this one piece of the puzzle encourages us to live peace. Our ego is not connected to the outcome. We can know or discover how to offer that support without becoming a part of the suffering. Through understanding the legitimate needs of another and responding with kindness, we act with compassion. We offer support for as long as it is needed, and then go on our way, allowing the person to maintain their boundaries and integrity.

True compassion is the outcome of a deep connection to the interdependence of us all. We are connected. We are one body of humanity. What we do to another we do to ourselves. Compassion for others grows out of compassion for our Self. Our responsible acts of kindness and compassion return to us in the form of the joy of helping another. They return to us when we need assistance and another (not necessarily the one we helped) is compassionate toward us.

In the early 1990's I was introduced by a dear friend to Kwan Yin, who is a bodhisattva of compassion. (I will explain what a bodhisattva is below.) In one of the stories describing her, she had an extremely difficult childhood which resulted in her deep compassion for others. Her name means "hearer of the cries of the world." There are shrines in her honor in Japan, Korea, China, and Taiwan. Kwan Yin is considered to be the feminine form of Avalokiteshvara, the bodhisattva of compassion of Indian Buddhism, who is said to have emanated from the tear of the Buddha. Worship of Avalokiteshvara was introduced into China in the third century. Both the female and male versions of this bodhisattva are said to be the embodiment of compassion.

A bodhisattva is a person destined for Buddha-hood, who chooses not to enter nirvana because they wish to continue to help others to alleviate suffering and find their own way to nirvana. When I first heard Kwan Yin's story, I was deeply touched by her profound compassion and care for humanity. I began to form the intention that I would become the embodiment of love and compassion. I asked for guidance from my Source and strongly believe that this prayer or intention is what has brought me to the work I do. As a Reiki Master/Teacher, offering meditation practices to others, and writing the messages that present themselves to me, making them available to anyone who has an interest in them, I believe that I am grounded in compassion. It is through compassion and kindness that we can bring peace to our world. Compassionately hearing the needs of the world and, responding to them with kindness are the keys to creating peace in our own lives and promoting it in society.

Seeing social injustice in our community, work place, or society and responding by first observing ourselves and how we treat others, and then by peacefully supporting change in the way people are treated, is another example of compassion. Compassion does not result in self-righteousness, but in right action. When we decide to take action against injustice, say racism for example, we must first take a very close look at our own actions and reactions toward people. When we understand that we are not perfect, that in all likelihood we hold prejudices against others, we know that it is time to change our own behavior. When we see that we are sometimes guilty of misunderstanding, or even mistreating, others based on race (or any other difference,) we know that we can change. It takes the work of compassion, both toward ourselves and toward those we have mistreated or misunderstood, to make the necessary changes.

Martin Luther King Jr., Mahatma Gandhi, and others who promote social change through peaceful action have taught that acts that promote peace are compassionate. Peaceful action depends on seeing the issue with compassion. When we see clearly, we can take a stand in a way that is meaningful and can produce the result of reducing the stigma that leads to injustice. We can see the burden born by others. We can see that only through change in our community members' understanding of people, will mistreatment be transformed to respect. We can take steps to help people understand that difference is not bad. We can remove fear by getting to know those who we think of as different from us. We can reach out and support people as they struggle against injustice. We can stand with them and make the changes first in our own lives, and then promote the changes necessary in our community. The best way to do this is through the practice of compassion.

We must communicate with those we see being mistreated. We must truly understand what is going on. It is extremely important that we understand what it is that the person we believe is oppressed wants to see changed. To see the issue and decide we know the answer without this step is not compassion. It can be patronizing. When we gain an understanding of the truth of a situation we can begin to help change society through compassion. Our compassion is needed not only toward those who are injured by the injustice, but also toward those who, in not understanding, are promoting injustice.

I have learned through many experiences that the best way to get over my own prejudices is to get to know people who I think are different from me. Once I really know someone, I care about them, about how they are treated, and about the challenges they face. I learned that the needs of gay, lesbian, bisexual, and transgendered people are exactly the same as mine by becoming friends with people who live these experiences. I learned that there is no need to be afraid of people of different races than mine by getting to know the people of those races. We are one body of humanity and our differences are what make life interesting and beautiful.

When I learned through experience that my lesbian friends needed to be able to support each other in a health crisis and didn't have the same rights I have with my husband, I knew that this must change. Compassion is what brought me the understanding of the need for change in our society. I know that I have more to learn. I also know that through acts of true compassion we can change the way people are treated. Change starts within. Then, through compassionate action, we can begin to change society.

Taking a public stand with others to promote fair and equal treatment of all people is a compassionate act. Allowing our stand to turn violent, self-righteous, and accusatory is not compassionate. When we work toward social justice, it does not serve us to degrade one part of society in order to uplift another. We all share our planet, our country, our community, and our block. When we open our compassionate eyes and minds to see the injustice, we can work through peaceful words and actions toward justice. It's easy to decide it's not our job, or to assume that someone else will take the challenge, or to believe that we cannot change our society. If, through compassion we really see injustice we must, in our own integrity, take a stand.

Reflections on My Journey with Compassion

I have often experienced the compassion of others. When I was ill friends did such things as taking my son to the dentist, giving me rides to or home from the hospital, preparing meals for my family, and probably most important, checking to see how I was doing. When it was imminent that our home was going to be flooded, people helped my family to move out so that most of our belongings were saved. When our home was rebuilt and the time came to return home, I had a broken shoulder, and people offered compassion by helping us move back and unpacking for us. This was all a great training ground for me to understand how to be compassionate toward others. My mother tells me that I have always been caring. (I blamed it on her for naming me Karen—it almost rhymes with caring!) As a child I would walk around the block to help an elderly woman thread sewing needles because she couldn't see well enough to do it herself, and she loved to sew. I also remember brushing an older woman's very long hair that she had never cut and could no longer brush by herself. Reflecting on that, I recognize that it was the practice of compassion that my mentor spoke of. I was able to see their need, help them the way I could, and go on with my life. I didn't take on their burdens; I just supported them in the way that I was able. I remember that I liked both of these women very much. I was young, and beginning to learn the ways of compassion toward others.

As an adult I have made some mistakes in the name of what I thought was compassion. I have sometimes ended up not being helpful at all. There is a fine line between supporting with compassion and enabling. When I have tried to fix another person's life for them I was not offering them compassion. I was taking over their circumstances, not respecting their journey and its lessons, and trying to make things the way *I* thought they should be. I have injured myself and some relationships with people because I thought I was being compassionate when, in actuality, I was trying to take away, or fix their problem. In one instance I ended up feeling taken advantage of, used, and miss-treated. In another I felt an ego boost because I had "solved" their problem. In neither case was I empowering the other person or actually helping them. My intentions were good, but my actions were misguided. Both of these individuals would have been better served if I had taken a few moments to really consider what was happening. I would have been more helpful if I had asked questions about the situation, understood what was really going on, and found out what kind of help they wanted. Then I could have assessed my own ability to help, understood whether what I wanted to offer was truly helpful, and made a decision based on understanding rather than assumption. I could have honored their integrity and my own by helping them see their own way through the problem. Supporting them as they took their own actions to correct their problems would have resulted in the truest form of compassion. There would not have been a sense of superiority on my part. Nor would there have been a sense that either of them owed me anything in return. I, therefore, would not have felt taken advantage of.

In the early years, as I began to understand injustice, working toward justice with compassion was challenging because it was much easier to get angry. When I react with anger I am likely to undo the work that has been done. In my country right now, immigration practices are highly unjust. Undocumented immigrants are called *illegal aliens*. While it is only a misdemeanor to be in this country without documentation, people's safety is compromised by prejudice. Undocumented people cannot feel free to ask for help from authorities because of the fear of deportation. Individuals can be the subject of crime, even violent crime, and not report it because of fear of deportation. This is not in the service of justice for all. Families can be torn apart as children born here are separated from parents, who were born elsewhere and came here seeking work, seeking good education for their children, seeking hope for their families. There is no compassion in our society's treatment of people who have come here for good reasons, are working at becoming a part of our communities, and do work that needs to be done.

This injustice raises the example of one of the ways I can encourage compassion in my community. By promoting sanctuary cities where authorities won't require proof of citizenship or a green card in order to come to the assistance of people in need, I am acting with compassion. By getting to know the people who are here trying to take care of their families, and learning to understand the injustices they experience, I can take peaceful and compassionate action toward change.

There are many injustices in our world. I can see that I can be instrumental in making changes so that my community is more compassionate. Through first understanding the injustice, then examining my own part in it, and gaining an understanding of what needs to change, I can begin to take action through compassion. This is part of my journey with compassion.

Reflections on Your Journey with Compassion

_____
_____
_____
_____
_____
_____
_____
_____
_____
_____
_____
_____
_____
_____
_____

"This is the work of compassion: to embrace everything clearly without imposing who we are and without losing who we are."

MARK NEGRO, *THE BOOK OF AWAKENING*

CHAPTER 5

Gratitude

The attitude of gratitude is the key to joy. Without gratitude we are incapable of feeling joyful. We can go about our lives unaware of the blessings around us. We can be blind to the beauty of nature, to the kindness of others, to our connection with the Divine, our inner light, or our higher Self. In this blindness we are not able to experience gratitude and joy. All it takes to change this is to notice. Notice the sunrise or sunset, notice when someone does something kind, or notice when you feel good. Then express your gratitude! You will find that as you begin to notice the positive things in your life, you will more often experience joy in living, and in being.

It is this attitude of gratitude that helps us to draw unto ourselves more of what we are grateful for—more kindness from others, more kindness from ourselves toward others. We begin to appreciate the small blessings of life. This gratitude, in turn shows us the greatest blessings in life. When we begin to actively appreciate our blessings, we connect with the people and things for which we are grateful. When we connect in this way, we enhance our experience of life and our ability to be a blessing in the lives of others.

Gratitude opens us to love, connection, and joy. When we are expressing our gratitude we notice the abundance in our lives, even if we are in a situation that does not seem to be abundant by society's standards. There is great abundance in nature. Love that goes unnoticed does not bring a sense of abundance, but when we notice that we are loved we feel bathed in abundance!

Living in gratitude promotes joyful peace within.

It is the times in life when I am most grateful that I feel the strongest connection to The Holy. When I sit with the feeling of gratitude and intentionally allow it to fill my being, I feel so close to Spirit that I am engulfed in it. I have had the experience of being in a discordant state of mind and then returning to gratitude. When I take the time to notice and then, in gratitude, express and feel deep appreciation, colors instantly become more vivid; connections with loved ones, more profound; scents more beautiful. In that moment, I am connected to the Divine in a deep and profound way and everything feels more real—more intense, more peaceful, more exciting.

Understanding that I am part of the wholeness of all that is, and engaging in gratitude helps me connect with others. When I am able to let go of the idea that I am separate from the Source of my being, from any person or thing in the world, the gratitude that fills me also helps me to be compassionate and forgiving toward others.

Gratitude is the glue of manifestation. When we are in a state of gratitude, we are capable of drawing to ourselves more of what we are grateful for. Or maybe we just enjoy it more, so it feels like there's more of it. Either way—what a gift!

We have gratitude for the *things* in our lives—cars, homes, electronic devices that make our lives easier, clothing, furniture and so on. We have gratitude for *people* in our lives, loved ones, family members, friends, and people we work with or see on a regular basis. We are grateful for nature, sunshine, trees, fire, water, oceans, animals, and air. The gratitude I am speaking of here includes much of this, and goes deeper.

What is that feeling of gratitude? It is not the feeling of attachment. Gratitude allows us to hold what we are grateful for, what and whom we love, with an open hand. Nothing in life is permanent. Life itself is not permanent. Our gratitude for the presence of these things and for people enriches our lives. If we become attached to things they can become burdens. Attachment is a concept that Buddhists work on. Attachment is the sense that we can't survive, go on, or function without the things or people we are attached to. When we are attached and things change, or seem to change, we become fearful and hang on tight to our idea of the things we're attached to. We hold on tighter and tighter to the old idea and can't see blessings in the changes—or forget the blessings in the presence of this person or that object in our lives.

For example, when our home was flooded in the Great Floods of Iowa in 2008, we lost our ability to live in our home. We had 40 inches of water in our single story dwelling. We had to move out, rebuild, and move back. I did okay with this. I remember saying to my husband, "A house is sticks and stones and bricks and mortar. We can have that somewhere else." Our home has been rebuilt. It is both more beautiful and more functional for us now, and I am very grateful for its beauty. As much as I enjoy living in this space, I hold it with an open hand. Experience has shown me that it can disappear in a day. I am not afraid. I am grateful for the opportunity to live here now, and confident that, should the need arise, I can move forward with strength and integrity into the next living situation my husband and I create.

Another example: When children come into our lives, we know that we don't own them, but we love them and want the best for them. We spend the first many years of their lives nurturing and teaching them. When we do this with an open hand, knowing that they will leave, that they will make decisions that we may not agree with, that they will form their lives in their own way, we can hold onto the love and let go of the attachment when the time is right.

Where does gratitude come from? This is a great question. In my experience gratitude sometimes comes as a surprise, but most often as a decision on my part. When it comes as a surprise—when I realize that I am grateful for an act of kindness or for a moment of joy—I can be filled with an overwhelming sense of gratitude. I feel happy, even ecstatic. It comes in a moment, unexpected and unbidden. Other times I make a decision to be grateful. It can still grow into an overwhelming sense of gratitude for life, for being, or for relationship. When I'm irritated at someone I love,

I have to remind myself what it is that I love about this person, and decide if that makes it easier to forgive the offense. Gratitude helps me move more quickly and freely into forgiveness.

I am grateful that nothing I ever do, that no mistake I will ever make, or have ever made, will separate me from the Source of my being. In that gratitude, I realize that mistakes made by loved ones won't separate me from my love for them. Then forgiveness comes more easily.

How do we tap into gratitude and transform our fears of loss into gratitude for what is—whatever is? Transformative thinking comes through self-awareness. When we notice that we are wrapped up in fear-based feelings of discontent, anger, jealousy, or greed, or in fear itself, we realize that in this state, we are not capable of gratitude. In this case it often seems impossible to turn the ribbon of emotions from fear-based anxiety or worry to a love-based sense of gratitude. It can take time and healing work to return to our sense of gratitude around what has caused these feelings.

In the case of discontent, we make changes by looking for what is available to be content with. Then we do the work of changing things so that we are content. That may mean changing something about our lives, or changing our attitudes about it. We may have to take a breath, to step back from a situation, and look at it with fresh eyes, seeing where fear has intruded and realizing our true gratitude.

Gratitude can be the answer to the fear-based sense that there isn't enough, that we are inadequate in some way, that life is too hard, or that our needs are not met. I understand that there will be times in all of our lives when these examples are true. If we take a moment when we feel this way to notice just one thing for which we can be grateful, we can turn around our thinking. Then we can begin to take positive actions to change things that need to change. If we're stuck in a sense of lack, or in loss, or in whatever sensation has us stuck in fear-based thinking we can use gratitude as the potion to energize change.

There are many gratitude exercises: you can write down five things every day for which you are truly grateful; you can start your day noticing the things that you are grateful for; you can tell people when you are grateful for their actions. Any activity that increases our awareness of the goodness in life is helpful.

How do we intentionally engage in the attitude of gratitude? Practicing gratitude can be a powerful tool for accomplishing living in gratitude. Some days it's more difficult than others to find this state of being in gratitude. It is my practice to do this no matter what else is going on in my life. I meditate every morning. My first thoughts are of gratitude for life, for where I am in the moment (home or away from home), for family, and love, for my understanding of Spirit. I move into gratitude for my body, for this temple of my soul. Most of all I am grateful for my deep connection to Spirit and my understanding of oneness with All. The gratitude I carry for the *things* in life is not as important or profound as gratitude that I am, that I exist, that I am connected to Spirit and to all of existence. Gratitude for people in my life is the energy behind what fires me up to be compassionate, to forgive, to live my life in ways that nourish, and to thrive. This deep sense of gratitude, that I cannot explain, connects me to the people I love, to the nature I enjoy, to doing what I need to do to heal my body, mind, and spirit, and to being a peaceful presence in the universe. It connects me to my work, to the purpose of what I do. Gratitude is the glue that holds it all together.

Reflections on My Journey with Gratitude

Gratitude has not always been my attitude. There have been times in my life when I was stuck in a malaise of sadness and fear. During the years when I was ill with intractable migraines it was difficult to find my way into gratitude. I was on disability. I felt like a drain on my family. I felt worthless as I missed important events in my children's lives. Sadness was a pretty dominant theme.

At one point I decided to go into counseling. The most powerful tool I learned from my therapist was to look at my thinking and change it. When I thought, "I can't," I looked at what I COULD do. When I thought negative thoughts about myself like, "I am unlovable because I'm sick," I remembered that I was loved, sick or not. I recalled that when I was feeling well, I did have fun and engage in life. When I felt like the illness would never end, I remembered that others who were sicker than I had regained their health.

I eventually learned the lesson to change my thinking. That is where my talk about turning the ribbon from fear to love, or from lack to gratitude, comes from. It took a lot of practice to change the way I thought, but it was worth the effort. I still have times when I have to remember and practice positive thinking.

There were times when I was so angry about something someone did that I was in a state of rage. One sunny morning this happened. I was on my way to work, very angry. At some point I decided that I was not going to let anger rule my day and looked for something to be grateful for. Amazingly and immediately, the sun seemed brighter, the sky bluer, the air fresher. Everything was better and all I had done was decide not to let anger take over and to notice what I could be grateful for. It was an amazing and affirming experience! It taught me a valuable lesson about life.

Now it is my habit to notice the beauty in life regardless of what else is going on. It has become a practice in gratitude that moves with me through my day. I begin in the morning with sitting in meditation, stating my gratitude for all that I am grateful for. I move into filling my life, my home, my surroundings with love, and then into sending love to all of the people in my life. Then I become silent and rest in the presence of Spirit, listening for ideas, filled with the lightness of love, gratitude, and joy. It's a great way to begin each day!

Here's a fun tale about an experience that surprised me and made me even more grateful. We needed new furniture when we were moving into a new home. We weren't sure what we wanted, and my husband didn't want to choose furniture, so I was wandering around a furniture store. I saw a living-room suite that I liked very much, and would work beautifully in our new home. It was beyond the budget, but I decided to sit and enjoy it for a few moments before moving on. As I sat there the sales person came to me and said that he had just learned that they were in competition with another store and he had to reduce the price of each piece by $100. That was exactly the amount over my budget the living-room suite was. I bought it then and there!

Would that have happened if I hadn't taken the moment to enjoy the furniture? The price would have gone down, but I would have moved on and not known it. I'm sure I would have found something that I liked, but I got what I wanted *because* I took a moment to enjoy it! We never know when our lives can change by taking a moment to notice, to enjoy a situation, and feel our gratitude.

Another time that I am overwhelmed with gratitude is when I'm with my children and/or my grandchildren. I cherish the time I have with each of them. I feel full of light and gratitude, happy and content. We don't have to be doing anything special, just being together does it for me. I notice it, I express it, and I enjoy it fully. There are a few friends who have this effect on me as well. The key is to notice—to express your sense of gratitude (silently or aloud) and immerse yourself in the experience. People around you will feel your joy and their lives will be touched by it too.

I am human. Not every moment is filled with gratitude, but now most are. Sometimes I feel tired or overwhelmed and get stuck. It can last for a few days, but I have learned to take a look at my attitude when I'm feeling this way and return to the attitude of gratitude. It changes things every time. I still have as much to do, I still feel tired, but I can tackle the jobs that need doing because I know that the result will be worth it, and I am grateful.

Reflections on Your Journey with Gratitude

_____
_____
_____
_____
_____
_____
_____
_____
_____
_____
_____
_____
_____
_____
_____
_____

"The single greatest thing you can do to change your life today would be to start being grateful for what you have right now. And the more grateful you are, the more you get."

— OPRAH WINFREY

CHAPTER 6

Integrity

Integrity implies wholeness. It means to live authentically—to be our authentic Self. Living according to our beliefs, according to the standards that come from within us, according to our understanding of what it means to be true to who we are and what we believe, is a large part of integrity. When we live with integrity we are aware of what we understand to be our purpose in life in the present moment, and we are living in ways that support that purpose. In order to be our authentic Self, we must first know our authentic Self. Through meditation, journaling, reading, conversation with others, worship, being in nature, and other methods, we come to know our deepest truth, the authenticity of our inner being. As we grow in our understanding, our authentic Self changes.

Integrity includes honoring what we are doing in the present moment, no matter what it is: washing dishes, taking out the trash, speaking in public, interacting with others, or being alone. Every moment is precious and deserves our highest integrity and our full presence.

When we embrace integrity in our way of being, we automatically bring peace into our lives. Because we are being true to our highest guidance, our Higher Self, we feel whole, one, connected, centered, and at peace.

Living in integrity promotes peace in our lives, in our hearts, and in the greater world around us.

One way to approach this rather elusive word it is to look at some of its definitions. In the Oxford dictionary, integrity is defined as "moral uprightness; honesty; wholeness; soundness." This would indicate that living in integrity means that we hold to the values that guide us (moral uprightness). It also implies that honesty is part of integrity, meaning that we are honest when we express ourselves in our words, actions, and deeds. It indicates a sense of wholeness in the sense that we are honest in all of our lives, in every situation, in every relationship. Dr. Usui, the man I talked about in Chapter 1, who brought Reiki into the world and who introduced the Reiki principles, stated this one as "do an honest day's work." For me this principle means far more than working eight hours for eight hours of pay. It means doing my best in each situation I encounter, being true to my belief system, and examining my motives to be sure that my actions are guided by compassion and, hopefully, promote outcomes that are for the highest good of all.

Practicing integrity requires that we be the internal observer of our motivations and actions. If we are pursuing a task for the betterment of our own financial situation, are we taking an action that embraces the criteria of "do no harm?" Is "do no harm" enough? When engaging integrity, whatever we do with our resources (time, energy, finances, thoughts, and ideas) is examined for moral uprightness. When attempting to change our lives for the better, will the steps we take be for the betterment of others as well? Will our actions cause lack or pain for someone else? Are our actions true to our authentic self? These are questions I have asked while working on this book, while teaching Reiki, and while seeking support for the non-profit organization I work with, along with other times in my life. These are questions I ask when I am trying to solve a conflict, express my feelings, or engage in discussion. This doesn't mean that we forfeit our own well-being. It means that whatever we undertake in our lives is guided by principles of fairness, equality, compassion, and honesty; by the principles in this book: forgiveness, confidence, compassion, gratitude, and integrity. It requires that we remember that we are a part of the wholeness of All That Is, and that our actions, interactions, and reactions have an effect on all others.

Where do the values of integrity come from? When do we find that our authentic Self is a peaceful caring being? Are these values always found through what our parents have taught us; through our religious beliefs; or through the mores of society? If we seek deeply within, questioning each answer to get to the core of our beings, will we eventually get to a natural, peaceful motivation within us, an understanding that we are all here to help one another? Is it human nature to nurture—to help, to be aware of the needs of others and try to do something about those needs?

Our own integrity requires that we honor the integrity of others. We know that there are people in the world whose inner peace is not, or at least appears not to be, disturbed by taking advantage of others. It's not possible to know the underlying motivation for others' actions. It does us no good to proceed through life, making judgments on how other people are living their lives, except to discern whether their actions are ones we want to emulate. What this kind of judgment accomplishes is yet another set of barriers between people. If we judge another's integrity we often assess whether we think they are as good as us. What a way to remove peace!

A sense of being better than anyone cannot help us create peace within ourselves or in our communities. If we hold up each person with acceptance of who they are at this moment on their life journey, knowing that they are doing what feels right to them, we let go of judgment and proceed to holding them in high regard, unconditional love.

How do we answer the question of where integrity comes from? Could it be a "millionth monkey" phenomenon? If enough people in the world can create deep and abiding peace within each of us will the world become a peaceful, compassionate, loving place? I believe that this is a possibility. It gives me the hope to continue moving forward with peace at my core, expressed through my being, my doing, and my thinking.

While it is certainly within the scope of this work to examine our own ulterior motives, our thoughts, and our actions, it is not for us to judge the motivation of others. Not everyone is living by these principles, and they would seem very foreign to some. It is our responsibility to do our best to live with integrity. If we engage in judgment of others, we are placing ourselves "above" or separate from them. Judgment of others will not promote peace either within ourselves, or in our world.

We reduce our own integrity and our understanding of another's through the very common practice of comparing. This is deeply ingrained in our societal mores. Comparing reduces our understanding of another's individual integrity because we are holding them to a standard that is external to them. We do this to ourselves as well, and it's not helpful in that capacity either. Comparing ourselves or others to each other to discern our—or their—"good-enough-ness" is harmful to us, to our communities, and to our understanding of integrity.

Integrity requires of us that we know our limits and act accordingly. We would not be acting in integrity if we made a promise to do something that we knew we did not have time for. We would not be acting in integrity if we promised to do things that are beyond our ability. So integrity requires that we limit our promises to what we can actually accomplish. Further, integrity requires that we be consistent. If we treat strangers with kindness, we must, in integrity, treat all strangers with kindness. If we set ourselves to being truthful, we have to be truthful all of the time—even when it's not easy or comfortable.

Integrity is challenging. We can't pick and choose when to have integrity. We either have it or we don't. That is a very black-and-white statement. There are times when our integrity is stronger than others, when we aren't quite able to live up to our own expectations. It is a quality that grows within us as we live our lives consciously; as we are the self-observer. I believe it is something that comes with maturity, but I could be wrong. Perhaps two-year-olds have tremendous integrity. When they don't want something, we know it! When they are unhappy, we know that! When they are happy we are aware of that too. They haven't learned to lie yet and so their integrity is intact. Perhaps integrity is a trait we are born with and in our socialization we learn to compromise it without understanding that's what we've done. That would suggest that our work is to return to the integrity and honesty of a child. Yet as we live our lives, and embrace the understanding that comes with growth, with experience, and with maturity, what we have learned becomes a part of our integrity.

The concept of integrity is challenging to discuss. We know what it's not. It's not manipulating situations to make ourselves look good without actually doing the work to *be* good. It's not lying or bearing false witness. It's taking responsibility for our own actions and words in all situations. But it seems to be more than that. It's the wholeness of it that is hard to express. Integrity, by its nature permeates every aspect of our lives. Relationships depend upon it. When we are in the process of creating, we will fail if we don't adhere to our own integrity and the integrity of what we are trying to create.

I think that integrity is the fifth of five principles because each of the first four is an aspect of it. The work of forgiving requires an honesty within that is integrity. Confidence requires that we examine the integrity of that which we have confidence in. Compassion requires that we honor the integrity of others as well as or ourselves. Gratitude is an expression of love and joy, and we can't be falsely grateful!

As with the other principles discussed in this book, reaching a point in our lives where we have true integrity, true authenticity, is a journey. Life will show us when we are not holding ourselves to integrity. We will find ourselves outside of our comfort zone. When we live with integrity, we embrace all that we are in the moment and live accordingly.

Reflections on My Journey with Integrity

One of the biggest integrity challenges in my life came when I realized that every day, as I walked down the street I was judging each and every person I encountered. My thoughts would go something like this: As I approached a person who was overweight my judgment could go either of two ways—"Do I look better than that?" or "How can that person live with themselves?" Approaching a person who was walking a dog—"I wonder if they clean up after that dog." Coming across someone who looked disheveled—"They must be homeless." And so on.

I am not at all proud of those days and I am glad to be constantly learning to let go of the habit. I have talked this over with many different people as I've struggled to change my thoughts and behavior to engaging compassion rather than judgment. Some people have said that the judgment that comes so easily is a way of protecting ourselves. Others have told me that it is natural to judge each and every person we encounter. I think it's learned behavior, although it was so deeply ingrained I'm not sure where I learned it. It's true that it could be a part of our socialization. At any rate, it doesn't help.

I have learned to change that judging voice by noticing that if I am one with every being, I am also the person I am judging. The only difference between me and any other person is the experiences we have had in life. A different decision, a different set of circumstances, a different genetic inheritance is the only thing that sets us apart. I learned that people are not always what they seem to be. Someone down on their luck may be brilliant. A head of a corporation may be lacking in common sense. There are many examples and I'll leave you to examine the conclusions you jump to by the appearance of people you encounter.

Learning to honor differences has been the most difficult lesson I have learned in my journey with integrity. I know that my own integrity is tied to the way I understand and hold the integrity of others. The differences in belief systems, cultural norms, preferences, behaviors, and communication are a few of the challenges to my understanding of the integrity of others. One of the most important lessons in my life has been to get to know individuals who fall into categories that I judged as different. Just spending time with people and learning that we all want the same thing has been an eye opener. Having friends in a committed homosexual relationship taught me the importance of their love, and the importance of understanding that they have exactly the same needs, and deserve the same rights that I have within my own marriage. Having friends who are people of color has opened my eyes to the many ways that they are profiled and, therefore, their lives can be unsafe.

The list could, and does, go on, but you get the idea. My own journey with integrity has been informed by experiences in understanding other people. Once I learn about the challenges each perceived difference between me and any other person makes, my own integrity requires me to challenge my assumptions and change my attitudes. This has definitely been a part of my spiritual journey. My ability to embrace the oneness of all humanity could not develop without growth in compassion and understanding, and a willingness to change my mind.

Another aspect of integrity is the honesty it requires of us. That means that when I did the work of forgiving that I talked about in the chapter on forgiveness, in integrity, I could no longer engage in the aspects of that anger that fed my ego. I had to stop talking about that person with the other person who was angry.

Integrity is a deeply important part of how we present ourselves to the world. If my belief system is part of who I am I cannot hide it. I must be honest in conversations with others about beliefs. Sometimes it's easier to say that I believe in a particular understanding of God. Explaining what I mean if I say the word God has been interesting. Some people look like they think I'm a little weird. Others seem interested, but don't want to go into depth. Still others want to know more. But I have learned that I cannot allow people to believe that my belief system is the same as theirs. This is especially important in my work as a Reiki Practitioner. Clients have assumed that, because of the insights I gain when I work with them, I pray in the same way that they do, or that my beliefs must be the same as theirs. At times I've had to talk with clients and explain that they are making assumptions about my belief system and that the god I believe in is energy, love, life force. That means that I don't necessarily pray the way that they do. I don't believe that I am more blessed or less blessed in any situation.

Reflections on Your Journey with Integrity

"Be the change you want to see."

MAHATMA GHANDI

Karen J. Fox

CONCLUSION

It is important to recognize that living these principles is a practice. By embracing forgiveness, confidence, compassion, gratitude and integrity, we continually seek ways to live more sincerely. It can be a daily challenge to live the principles we have discussed. If we berate ourselves for any missteps or failures, we are already taking ourselves out of peacefulness. It's much more helpful to correct ourselves with compassion toward our own actions than it is to degrade ourselves for our mistakes. When we discern our own behaviors or thoughts that are opposed to these principles, we can gently correct ourselves. Sometimes the correction will require asking for forgiveness, having an open conversation with someone, changing our behavior, or stepping back to think things through. It usually requires all of these actions, and sometimes more. As we engage in the practices of forgiveness, confidence, compassion, gratitude, and integrity, we engage in a life guided by love—a life lived peacefully.

We are continually challenged to recognize that we are as capable of mistakes and misjudgments as anyone else. We grow in our understanding and expression of living peace as we practice it. We start with the intention, and then we practice, practice, practice. We correct ourselves along the way, and eventually we find that, at least most of the time, we are living peace. When this happens and we are holding ourselves to integrity, we are recognizing our responsibility to live our lives guided by principles that promote peace.

Peace in the world begins with peace in the heart. That means peace in each heart. To create a peaceful world, we must first create a peaceful life for ourselves. Our sense of peacefulness is nourished when we are at peace with others. This implies that forgiveness and compassion promotes peace in our world. Peace is not an isolated, internal emotion, secluded from our environment. To be at peace with myself I must know that, in my own integrity, I am honoring the integrity of all others. When I have peace in my mind and in my heart, I am promoting peace in the world.

The commonly heard statement, "may peace prevail on earth," is a good example of how we ignore our own responsibility for creating peace now. When we make this statement, are we recognizing that peace will only prevail when we find peace within? Are we abdicating responsibility by saying, "*may* peace prevail" instead of saying, "*peace prevails*" on earth—within me, within others? If we individually engage in living peace and we talk about it, share it, spread it in whatever way we can, peace prevails in us, and is spread to others. I believe that peace can expand, and that affirming that it prevails in this moment within me and around me helps to manifest it everywhere.

Live peace.
Be peace.
Share peace.

ACKNOWLEDGEMENTS

There are so many people who have influenced the writing of this book and deserve my gratitude.

First, I want to thank my family, my husband, Charles Eastham, for his support and encouragement, as well as for the long talks we've had about principles that I found challenging to articulate. I am grateful to my three children Abbey, Aaron, and Ashley, who have taught me many lessons as they grew into adulthood.

Deep gratitude goes to all of the Reiki students who have asked the questions that inspired the thought behind understanding these principles. A huge thank you goes to my Reiki Master/Teacher, Mary Lukas, who introduced me to Reiki, which was the beginning of this journey.

I also want to thank Jeet Saini for her support, Nazan Aksan, Lisa Bormann, Lily French, Miriam Kashia, and Lynn Zimba for reading, re-reading, and offering their feedback.

I would also like to express my appreciation of the many lessons learned while studying with the late Harold Barlow, my mentor and friend.

All of you, and others unmentioned, but not forgotten, have supported me on this journey. I am deeply grateful.

1. *A Complete Book of Reiki Healing*, Mendocino, CA, B. Muller a7 H. Gunther, Liferhythm, 1995.

2. When I use the words Spirit, All that Is, God, Universe, please insert the word that works best for you when thinking about a higher power.

3. *The Four agreements,* Miguel Angel Ruiz, M.D. 1997

4. *Women Who Run With the Wolves: Myths and Stories of the Wild Woman Archetype,* Balentine Books, New York, 1992, Clairissa Pinkola Estés, Ph.D.